FRAGMENTS

From

the Teachings

of

MEISHU-SAMA

Johrei ✤ *Fellowship Version*

"LIGHT" written by **MEISHU-SAMA**

MEISHU-SAMA
(MOKICHI OKADA)

Fragments

From
the Teachings
of

Meishu-sama

Johrei ✥ *Fellowship version of*
Fragments From the Teachings of Meishu-sama
Revised Edition

© 1998 by Johrei Fellowship
All rights reserved
Published by Johrei Fellowship
Torrance, CA 90504
Printed in the United States of America

Johrei® and the Izunome symbol ✥® are
registered trademarks of Johrei Fellowship

First edition copyright 1965
Printed in Atami, Japan

Printed 1995 USA

PREFACE

Fragments From the Teachings of Meishu-sama is a compilation of talks given by Meishu-sama to Johrei ministers and members who gathered from many areas in Japan. Because the illuminated concepts and ideas for the Age of Light revealed to him were profound and universal in nature, they needed to be interpreted in a simple manner.

It was an inspiration and a privilege to be in his presence and to listen to his revelations. His followers were happy to undergo any inconvenience or hardship in order to hear him. His love, sincerity and wit were unique. They are, however, difficult to convey in writing.

This book is published especially for those who wish to learn more about Meishu-sama's approach to a healthier, happier, more harmonious life in the Age of Light we are now entering, and for those who desire to dedicate themselves as channels to serve God and humanity.

In meditating upon these truths, their deeper spiritual meaning will be discerned. They will prepare the reader for the ever increasing vibratory rate of the Age of Light. We trust the reader will incorporate these Teachings into daily life as did Meishu-sama.

Inspired by the revelations which began unfolding in the year 1926, Meishu-sama founded a group based on spiritual truth in 1935. However, persistent persecution on the part of government agencies resulted in the termination of its public religious activities. It was not until 1945 that religious freedom was established in Japan and the spiritual movement reorganized.

Meishu-sama devoted the ten years preceding his transition to writing articles, publishing books and periodicals, and training ministers and leaders. He also created centers of beauty — prototypes of Paradise on Earth as revealed to him. One of these has an art museum in which rare art objects from his own collection are displayed. Additional art museums will be built as prototypes are constructed throughout the world.

In *Fragments* we find gems of truth and words of wisdom. May they expand each person's spiritual awareness and serve as valuable guides in the critical years ahead.

CONTENTS

PREFACE 1

1 *FROM DARKNESS INTO LIGHT* 5

Cosmic Cycles 7

Divine Drama 8

Divine Light Versus Tenets 10

2 *PURIFICATION* 15

Increased Light—Accelerated Purification . . 17

Suffering: A Form of Purification 18

Law of Spiritual Affinity and Purification . . . 20

Explanation of Misfortunes and Accidents . . . 23

Greater Mission—Greater Purification 25

Soil and Plant Impurities, Floods, Crime,

and the Transitional Period 26

3 *JOHREI* 31

Consecration in Channeling Johrei 33

Importance of Humility in Johrei 34

Spiritual Attunement 35

Understanding and Right Attitude 36

4 *WISDOM* 39

Awareness, Wisdom, Deadlock 41

Joy, Time, Order 42

Glory of Faith 45

Common Sense in Religion 47

Trust in God Versus Bondage 48

Contents

5 SERVICE 53

    Our Mission 55

    Purpose of the Divine Light Program 56

    God's Laws and Service 57

    Cosmic Credits 58

    Spiritual Atmosphere 59

    Membership Governed by Spiritual Law 60

    Be Guided in Expanding the Work 62

    Do Not Be Too Easygoing 65

    Rely on God 66

    God's Co-Workers 66

6 DAIJO, SHOJO, IZUNOME 69

    Daijo, Shojo, Izunome 71

    "Good" and "Evil" Are Relative 74

    Conflict Between "Good" and "Evil" 75

    Judge Not 77

    On Love 78

    Broadmindedness 79

    Love of Humanity Is Love of Life 81

    Freedom in Religion 82

    Be a Good Listener 83

    Yield That You May Conquer 85

1

From Darkness Into Light

Cosmic Cycles

*W*e live in a boundless, mysterious, but orderly universe which seems to evolve and revolve in cycles. A cycle is a period of time at the end of which certain aspects or motions of the heavenly bodies are repeated; a period of years or of ages; or recurring periods in which certain phenomena occur which, in turn, interrelate with the whole of life. There is the cycle of orbits in the heavens, the cycle of the seasons, of day and night. There is also the cycle of ages.

Changes take place on a small scale, an intermediate scale, and on a large scale; minor or major cycles may occur every ten, one hundred, one thousand, three thousand, ten thousand years, and so on, continuously recurring within the eternal flow of time. Truly the universe is infinitely mysterious—so mysterious it is beyond our present comprehension.

After an age of approximately three thousand years of comparative darkness, we are now in the dawn of the Age of Light. It is such an unprecedented change that it is difficult to grasp its full import. It is a turning point which none of our ancestors were privileged to experience. How fortunate are we who live at this time to even partially understand the real significance of the change and to have the means, through Johrei, of making the transition easier for everyone by serving God and humanity.

Divine Drama

*G*od's plan is working out in a unique way. It may be called a divine drama in which we of this age are all participants. Unless we realize this we shall be at a loss to know how to interpret the momentous happenings of our times and to understand that, as reconstruction advances, destruction also increases.

In any drama there are virtuous characters and wicked ones. Nearly always the virtuous are harassed by the wicked, but after they have been mercilessly tormented for a long time, the play usually ends with the good victorious. This is a happy finale. God's divine drama, cosmically ordained and now unfolding on the world stage, seems to follow a similar pattern. The present cyclic change is of inconceivable magnitude. If we but will, we can be intelligent observers as well as participants. Our appreciation of this unprecedented happening will be in proportion to our enlightenment and capacity to understand.

As the Age of Light advances and the spirit of fire increases, sickness, or purification, will also increase. More and more calamities such as war and natural catastrophes may occur, until the world will experience a time of terror. Generally speaking, our members may play the part of onlookers in scenes of war. But in scenes of sickness they will have active roles. To play a role serving humanity is far better than to play in scenes of violence or destruction.

The law of life demands that we live our lives constructively. We are in the dawn of the Daylight Age. As it advances and the spirit of fire becomes more intense, the baptism by fire will increase correspondingly; that is, the purifying power of the Light will become stronger. According to the law of affinity, as the unseen spiritual realm undergoes intense purification, those in the physical realm whose spiritual bodies are excessively clouded will find it difficult to endure the stepped-up purifying frequencies. Only those sufficiently cleansed may survive. Some of our members also may have difficulty during the time of the great purification. Therefore, we must endeavor to be prepared spiritually and physically if we are to pass through it with comparative ease.

This great cosmic drama has been referred to as the "Last Judgment." Our planet is the stage on which the breathtaking performance is being enacted. So great a drama could not be experienced at any other time. The conflict between good and evil is developing in a very complicated manner, until at last evil will be vanquished.

There have been more wicked actors than good actors. Those who play wicked parts are really to be pitied. The great love of God will save as many as possible, however, by working through the sincere channels of the divine Light. Johrei members feel called to serve as these channels.

Divine Light Versus Tenets

It is not creeds but divine Light which changes people.

People who consider this movement an ordinary religion often ask why it does not have specific tenets. I do not believe they are important. Tenets are doctrines and precepts; they cannot save people. Since ancient times nearly all religions have had their creeds, some of them well-considered, elaborate ones. Have they succeeded in perfecting the world?

In a novel I read recently, the author had one of his characters say in effect, "When I was young, I attended Bible class and one day we discussed miracles. Some believed in them; others did not. The discussion developed into a hot debate. Since I could not believe in miracles myself, upon reaching home I tried to strike from the Bible all references to them. But, when I read it without these passages, I found it to be merely a book of morals."

This is interesting. And, it is true! If religion consisted of doctrines only, it would offer no more than moral standards. These are not enough. In addition to moral principles, religion makes available to us the awareness of the great mystic and miracle-working power at work in the universe which cannot be explained by mere logic. The efficacy of religion lies in the tangible use of this mystic power. The more miracles a religion evidences, the more valid it may be considered.

Let me explain it in this way: Commandments alone are like laws enacted to prevent crimes. Laws are designed to maintain the established order of society and to impose penalties when they are violated. Many religions are founded upon commandments. The oldest of the well-known ones are the Ten Commandments given to Moses. During the Dark Age they were essential. But, "You must do this" or "You must not do that" implies penalties— spiritual penalties if not physical ones.

Threats and penalties are not the best way to keep a person from doing evil. An alcoholic probably will not abstain from drinking simply because the person is told that alcohol is bad for him or her. A far better way is to dispel the clouds from the spiritual body, raising the person to a level where divine nature will awaken within and cause the person to have a natural dislike for alcohol, or for wickedness, as the case may be.

It is the inclination to do evil or to act dishonestly that has to be eliminated, because the person inclined to corrupt practices has a preference for them. For example, to get money by dishonest means often seems more of a challenge than to earn it honestly. In this case, a person's divine or primary nature is in a weakened state, while the lower or secondary nature is strong and the soul is on a low plane. When the soul is on a higher plane, a person is unable to do these things.

Until people are no longer on this low level of consciousness, it is dangerous to be without legal regulations and penal institutions. In spite of strong enforcement of our regulatory laws, there are many bent on breaking them. This sometimes includes people in high office and social position, people who are looked upon as great personages. Social status or political office does not necessarily indicate spiritual development.

Furthermore, merely to abstain from doing evil because of the threat of penalty or criticism is not enough. Only when the individual reaches the plane where he or she has no desire to do wrong, where laws and regulations are not the deterrent, when the person finds delight in doing good, has the person awakened to his or her true state.

People cannot immediately reach the higher levels, but can do so step by step. While tenets are necessary, to an extent, the ultimate objective is higher than that. This movement endeavors to raise the individual to a more enlightened state of consciousness.

The invisible Light of God, channeled through Johrei, reaches the inner soul and transforms it, even when received with a skeptical attitude. It awakens the divine nature in people by bringing it into direct contact with the Light of the spirit. This is why the Johrei spiritual path is not an ordinary religion.

From the material point of view, this may be difficult to understand. But when the effect of Johrei is experienced, the divine Light of God is recognized. Even those who place great importance upon intellect cannot but awaken to the power of spirit over matter, and bow their heads in reverence.

2

Purification

Fragments From the Teachings of Meishu-sama

Increased Light—
Accelerated Purification

*I*t is vital that we come to realize that what we have termed sickness is but nature's process of restoring the rhythmic balance we call health, and that it is associated with the dispelling of the clouds accumulated on the spiritual body. The physical body must throw off its toxins—inherited, ingested, acquired or generated in whatever manner—in order that its functions may not be impaired. The discomfort or illness experienced is the unpleasant indication of the natural discharge of these poisons.

As the Age of Light advances and the intensity of the Light increases, purification will become more severe in corresponding degree. The raising of the vibratory rate through Johrei and through service will modify the severity by progressively dispelling the spiritual clouds, thus preparing one for the more intense Light without having to undergo too sudden or severe a purification.

In the coming Age of Light, the Light will be intense and direct, like the rays of the sun at midday.

An increase of purification can already be observed in every field, and this will become more and more severe. Everything false, wicked and impure will be brought to the surface and eliminated. There will be more physical illness, natural calamities, accidents, financial crises, and so forth. This general purification of the planet is what is meant by the "Last Judgment." We will gradually see it become a reality. Those who have been sufficiently freed from their impurities will be better able to adjust to this intense, direct Light. For those who have little or no spiritual understanding it will be a time of great tribulation instead of the fulfillment of God's plan it actually signifies.

Suffering: A Form of Purification

urification is governed by the law of affinity, as are all other processes. Wherever clouds or vibrations of a detrimental nature accumulate, an activity to dispel them occurs by natural law. This pertains not only to disorders of the physical body but includes misfortunes, miseries, accidents and natural disasters. It is not by chance that these occur; they are caused by the thoughts and deeds of people. When we come to understand this, we begin to see the reason for our misfortunes.

The big flood in the Kyushu area in Japan in 1953 was a result of an accumulation of impurities which gave rise to this great purification. Natural calamities such as typhoons and floods are calamities made by people; they are brought about by the wrong thinking and doing of the people. Before we decry our misfortunes and sufferings, realize that it is we who have caused them, and that we can blame no one else.

The majority of people, unaware of this, believe the cause of the misfortunes to be outside themselves. They overlook their own faults and place the blame upon Mother Nature, other people, society, education or the government. Often people in leading positions hold and advance the same erroneous viewpoint. This is a great fallacy. It causes many people to be filled with resentment which, in turn, results in additional clouds or toxins.

Many people drive themselves into the proverbial corner. In extreme cases they even commit murder or suicide, incurring further serious spiritual consequences. Ignorance of the true reasons for our misfortune and suffering causes the vicious circle to continue.

Law of Spiritual Affinity and Purification

urification takes on different forms because of the difference in causation. For example, when clouds are formed by pecuniary or material sins such as theft or embezzlement which causes loss to others, or living beyond one's means and the like, they are often eradicated by subsequent material losses. If we take other examples, such as losses due to fire, fraud, failure in business, large expenditures for illness and the like, we see they also are atonements for wrongs of a material or pecuniary nature.

There are many instances of "prodigal sons" who squander huge legacies. Unconsciously they are atoning for the spiritual clouds accumulated by their ancestors. In such cases, the spirit of an ancestor often chooses one of the descendants to perform the mission of purifying the family of its clouds, so the family line may prosper and not die out. It would be useless, therefore, to try to reform such an individual and change his or her way.

In the case of two sons, one prodigal and unmanageable, the other "well-behaved," the one brother would seem bad and a discredit to his family from the ordinary viewpoint. However, when considered from the spiritual viewpoint, it is not so. The one brother is performing the mission of purifying the spiritual clouds of his family line. Thus, it is not possible to decide the good or the bad of things from the human viewpoint alone.

In sickness, too, there are reasons for the various conditions, depending upon the clouds formed. Wrong acts which cause the guilty person to avoid another's eyes often are purified through some kind of eye trouble. Hurtful, cynical or spiteful words painful to hear may find purification through ear or tongue trouble. Doing something to cause headaches to others can bring headaches to the doer. To express one's talents through arms and hands at the expense of others may cause purification through arm or hand difficulties.

Thus, a purification of the spiritual clouds is inevitable sooner or later, in conformity with the law of spiritual affinity. Whether or not one escapes punishment by society's law, one cannot escape the divine law, which is absolute.

Sincere people receiving and channeling Johrei may experience severe purifications. Strangely, the more dedicated they are, the more severe the purifications sometimes appear to be. Unless their faith is strong, they may waver. However, this is a most important time. While God's blessings will reward them for their sincerity, their spiritual clouds must first be dispelled to a certain degree, in the same way an unclean container must first be cleaned before it can be used for wholesome food. If they endure their suffering patiently, they will find themselves rewarded far beyond their expectations.

For some twenty years I was burdened with a huge debt. No matter how hard I tried to repay it, I did not succeed in doing so. My human self sometimes felt like giving up, but by 1941 I was able to repay it. The very next year, to my great surprise, an unexpectedly large sum of money came to me.

Also, it has been noted that a certain person, after suffering losses through fire, became more prosperous. His fortunes took a turn for the better upon his purification by means of the fire. The city of Atami, too, became much more prosperous after the big fire of 1950 than it had been before.

What is good is good, of course. But what seems to be disastrous or unfortunate is also good, since it serves as a purifying process, and when it is over everything will be better. The same truth applies to disease. The person who comes to regard all suffering in this light will have attained much spiritual enlightenment and peace.

Of course, this can apply only to someone who has true faith in God. The sufferings of one with little or no faith may merely give birth to more suffering. The more impatient a person is, the worse the situation usually becomes, and finally it may have reached ruinous proportions. The secret of happiness lies in one's understanding and acceptance of the law of spiritual affinity and purification.

Explanation of Misfortunes and Accidents

A cabinet maker told me, "One night last November, I heard the shrieking of a siren in a dream. It awakened me and I hurriedly got up to see what was happening. I found that a fire, caused by smoldering ashes, had broken out in my factory. The fire was extinguished before it could spread and the damage was slight. I am very grateful for the protection I experienced that night. But recently similar accidents have happened in my family, one after another. I wonder about the meaning of these events."

Some things seem predestined. The general blueprint for this life was established by the way we thought and acted, progressed or regressed, in previous embodiments. However, these pre-established blueprints can be modified for better or worse, depending upon the way we live *now*. Our misfortunes may be lessened and even eliminated altogether with God's divine assistance through service in obedience to God's will.

By living a dedicated life, the yukon [a person's spiritual counterpart in the spiritual realm] will eventually reach the place where physical misfortunes are reduced to mere bad dreams or eliminated altogether.

It is essential that the purification of the spiritual body continue as long as necessary. We must come to the realization that all suffering is for our ultimate cleansing. And do not forget that the greater the individual's mission is, the more intense the purification must be.

Greater Mission–
Greater Purification

A Johrei member who suffered one misfortune after another questioned why he was subject to severe financial, mental, and spiritual purifications, when his sincere desire was to devote his life to Johrei expansion work and in service to God.

It was explained to him that the great amount of clouds accumulated prior to such dedication must be dissolved.

Another reason is that those who have a greater mission than the average person undergo greater purification as a rule, and it is usually more severe. But through trust in God, miracles and blessings come to sustain them, to give them strength. Conditions gradually change and brighter, better phases appear. They are then able to do the works that are of special significance in the cosmic plan.

As long as there are clouds on the spiritual body, a cleansing is necessary, and the process of purification takes on various forms. Accept certain discomforts as natural companions to the physical, mental and spiritual "cloudcleansing," and know that our spiritual beings are thereby elevated to a higher plane of awareness.

Soil and Plant Impurities, Floods, Crime, and the Transitional Period

*T*he spirit of fire increases as the Age of Light advances. It is a purifying spiritual energy which influences the physical side of life in proportion to its intensity.

Reports from members refer to the fact that when receiving Johrei they often feel an emanation of heat, and sometimes perspire. This shows that the Light, though spiritual, does affect us physically. The increase in spiritual fire affects all phases of life in one way or another.

A startling effect on crops is seen in the increase of insects which manifest to consume the plant toxins. Farmers, not realizing this, use more and more kinds of chemical fertilizers which, in turn, give rise to more and more toxins and noxious insects. Different types of insects appear as different chemical fertilizers are used. Farmers, to combat these pests, then use poisonous insecticides, which give rise to insects of a more vicious nature. This tendency is increasing with every year. It is similar to the increase in the variety and number of human diseases as more and stronger drugs are used. By a law of nature, noxious germs or insects appear spontaneously as plants absorb the fertilizers which are toxic to them. According to the same law, the toxins must be eliminated. To accomplish this, nature relies on their being consumed. However, the insects not only ingest the toxins but also parts of the plants as well, and the plants then weaken or die.

The physical world is governed by self-regulatory laws. Wherever questionable or harmful matter accumulates, a corrective activity automatically strives to eliminate it. Therefore, when human beings upset the balance of nature with chemicals, purifying activities occur according to natural law.

During the Age of Night the purifying power was weak, and that is why chemicals were temporarily effective. But now that the spirit of fire is increasing, purification acts more quickly and with greater severity.

Let us consider the meaning of floods. The soil impurities caused by chemical fertilizers and insecticides naturally result in a cleansing action on the part of nature, in an effort to wash away these impurities. Because of the ever increasing chemical pollution, we shall experience more frequent floods and other unprecedented happenings. The fundamental principle of this applies to everything.

Disease also comes under this principle. The ingestion of substances foreign to the body increases toxins, then by further using unnatural chemicals and poisons to suppress the conditions so caused, they become the cause of still more and worse toxins, calling for even more severe purifications.

Germs arise to help eliminate the impurities accumulated within our bloodstream. In 1952, Japan had a considerable increase in certain diseases, the death rate from encephalitis alone being twelve times higher than in 1951.

We have corresponding activities in the social realm. Wicked people appear because of the accumulation of clouds which have been created by wrong social conditions. People's mistakes cause the aggregate spiritual body of society to become clouded over. The existence of wicked people is a logical consequence of the misuse of spiritual laws. The torments and sufferings they cause constitute a form of purification.

Their activities increase the clouds, however, and result in developing still more wicked people. As long as there is social corruption in general, there will be this vicious circle of conditions producing evil individuals, who themselves cause more terrible people to appear.

During the Age of Night, evil was suppressed by evil because the Light was weak. But now, as we enter the Age of Light and the spiritual fire becomes more and more intense, suppressive methods will lose their effectiveness. All dishonesty, vice and other evil activities will gradually come to light, just as all toxins will be dissolved and eliminated. The entire world will then realize that the only way to attain a true and happy society is to rely on the Light of God for spiritual elevation and the elimination of wrong conditions.

Fragments From the Teachings of Meishu-sama

3

Johrei

Consecration in Channeling Johrei

*J*ohrei is the name given to the channeling of a spiritual energy or divine Light to purify one's spiritual body and awaken one's divine nature. It prepares an individual to pass through the coming critical period, sometimes called the "Last Judgment."

The power of Johrei varies to some extent with each individual. Although all members wear the Sacred Focal Point through which the divine Light emanates, when the Light is channeled by one of deeper spiritual understanding, it is stronger and more effective. Its effectiveness may change even with the same person from time to time.

The Johrei Light itself is always powerful to the same degree, but it is influenced by the dedication, sincerity, humility, love and faith of the channel. The importance of attitude and thought during the channeling cannot be overemphasized.

It is important to be completely at ease, with arm, elbow and hand fully relaxed and the mind in a peaceful state in order that the flow may not be impeded.

The way the Sacred Focal Point is handled, too, makes a difference in the effectiveness of the Light. Great care must be taken to prevent interference with its vibratory power.

Importance of Humility in Johrei

*T*hose who have just finished the membership course and are not yet sure whether they can truly channel the divine Light often experience remarkable results. Should this, instead of making them grateful, give rise to false pride and cause them to think, "I am pretty good now," they may be surprised to find their ability to channel the Johrei power becoming weaker. When conceit is present, the power of Johrei is distorted.

Although it is good to have full trust in God and confidence in oneself, it is important to realize that we are only instruments in God's Divine Light Program.

Spiritual Attunement

here are times, when channeling Johrei to a seriously ill person, without much effect, that members find a specific additional prayer for God's help brings the desired result. Johrei is prayer in action, and we must always rely on God when channeling. Johrei is not merely a method, a technique, or a treatment, so if we feel the channeling is not effective, we must discover in what respect we are not in accord with the law and thus not attuned to the infinite source.

When we attune ourselves to God, our prayers will be answered.

Understanding and Right Attitude

Many ask, "Is Johrei effective whether one believes in it or not?" The answer is both "yes" and "no," although it is true that Johrei works regardless of belief. Someone who does not understand the channeling of the Light by means of Johrei may be helped, even though the person is skeptical about it. However, the circumstances differ for those who have had results from Johrei and have been given the opportunity to gain an understanding of its true meaning.

The law is immutable and everything works logically. A person who has not experienced Johrei and receives it skeptically, perhaps even arguing against it, may be excused for his or her attitude, as this is quite natural. But if, after reading the literature, taking the course, and experiencing its benefits, a person still has misgivings, Johrei may not work effectively. Thus it is that beginners, though doubtful, can experience gratifying results, while others may not.

People sometimes question the repeated purifications and wonder about their meaning. It is necessary and natural that the many layers of accumulated clouds, manifested as toxins, be eliminated, and so they are dissolved one after another. However, if there are repeated purifications of a stubborn and weakening nature, there may be a deeper spiritual reason. It may happen if there is a lack of gratitude, which limits the inflow of the divine Light. When we come to see the logical manner in which divine law operates, both cause and effect become more clearly understood.

Johrei is not merely another technique to be applied for the healing of physical ailments. The main purpose is to awaken the soul to the power of God and God's Light, which can change self-centered lives into God-centered ones.

4

Wisdom

Awareness,
Wisdom, Deadlock

P eople often ask, "Why did such and such a thing have to happen?"

When we look more deeply into the factors responsible for undesirable events, we can usually discover points which were counter to the natural laws involved. Things do not go smoothly unless everything we undertake is in accord with universal law.

When confronted with deadlocks, if we approach the problems calmly and prayerfully, we usually find the causes of our difficulties. Should we fail to discover in what respect we are not conforming to law, it may be because our spiritual bodies are excessively clouded and our discernment thus dulled.

As the Light received through Johrei and the reading of the revelations dispel the clouds and lift the spiritual vibration, we will come to understand the deeper meanings, and the cause of any deadlock will be seen. As soon as we are in accord with the law, the procedure will be smooth. It is important to know the law in any given situation and how to comply with it, to be alert and able to make adjustments.

Wisdom is gained through an extended awareness. It is when we attain this awareness that we can proceed more nearly in accord with divine law and accomplish whatever we undertake with comparative ease, greater efficiency and, eventually, perfection.

Joy, Time, Order

*W*ork done with a spirit of *joy* is done well and with ease. When we laboriously undertake something we do not feel like doing, we make little progress. I do my work in a spirit of play, like a hobby, never laboriously. It is my hope that Johrei channels will adopt such a spirit in their undertakings. It is of great advantage.

Many people see nothing wrong in expending great effort in what they do. They consider it natural, even feel proud of it. I, too, sometimes overdo without being aware of it until things begin to go wrong, and I say to myself, "I have been trying too hard." Then I stop and do something else. Too much effort seldom brings good results. The more smoothly and easily we are able to proceed, the greater our efficiency. The same principle applies in giving Johrei. Channeled in a spirit of joy, the results will be good. The better the results, the more delighted we will be.

Another important factor to consider is *time*. No project should be undertaken prematurely. If the proper moment is not at hand, we need to have the wisdom to perceive it, for no matter how worthy the project, it will not turn out well.

Still another important aspect which affects the outcome of our endeavors is *order*. We may undertake to carry out a plan thinking that we have taken everything into consideration and that the work will proceed smoothly. Contrary to our expectation, we find obstructions.

When we review the matter carefully, we find that we did not proceed in the proper order. As soon as we follow the law of order, everything goes smoothly.

Spiritual perception is important because it so greatly affects the outcome of any endeavor. Those who have achieved this insight quickly get to the pith and point of things.

Let us consider Johrei. When results are not encouraging, the fault may lie in the attitude with which Johrei is channeled or received. Perhaps the spirit of prayer is lacking in the one who is channeling it. Or, perhaps it is being given to a person whose family is opposed to Johrei. The action of the Light is then lessened, for the unsympathetic attitude of even one person can affect the result. The spiritual cords connecting family members are strong and exert a powerful influence.

After spiritual insight has been attained, when things do not work out well the reason will quickly reflect upon the mirror of the mind. This is an important point often overlooked. God's laws govern things according to circumstances. In every case success depends upon spiritual awareness as well as upon the specific situation.

The best way to cleanse the mirror of the mind and keep it clear is through Johrei and its Teachings. Sometimes a person finds, to his or her surprise, that when the literature is read again and again, profound wisdom is discovered and new inspiration received. This is due to the fact that in the beginning, the mirror of the mind is clouded. As the spiritual body is purified, the deeper import of the Teachings emerges.

Glory of Faith

There is a certain piquancy to everything in the world about us. All of the many forms of life, and all objects as well, have and impart a certain flavor of their own. If this flavor or individual zest were missing from our lives, the world would be so colorless, so inane, we would lose all desire to live. Our attachment to life, to a great extent, is due to the enjoyment of our sense perceptions.

There is a glory in true faith. However, people differ in their beliefs. Strange as it seems, there are religions which generate fear. Those who follow such religions are afraid of God, live according to rigid regulations, and are severely restricted by commandments. There is no happiness or freedom for people who live under a cloud of fear such as this.

True faith makes for serenity of mind and a happy life. When we attain this state, we perceive the love of God in the sun, the moon, the stars, in the beauty of nature, the songs of birds and the perfection of flowers. We recognize God's beneficence in the abundance with which God supplies our every need. We sense our oneness with all life — not only with people but with nature, with the plant and animal life all about us. This is religious ecstasy. In that tranquil and happy state of mind, upon having done our best in any situation, we have perfect trust in God.

When I am faced with a difficult problem which seems to defy solution in spite of my best efforts, I turn to God in perfect trust for help and guidance. I release my problem to God's wisdom and wait until the answer presents itself. I can say from experience that, even though a prospect looks dark in the beginning, the result is always better than anticipated. I also dream big dreams and pray to God for help in bringing them to pass. Through God's own ways and wisdom, I am blessed beyond my dreams. It is indeed wonderful.

Once in a while I encounter something, the prospect of which is so disheartening it weighs heavily on my mind. I say to myself, "This must be a prelude to something good, a blessing in disguise." Then I wait for God to clarify the problem. Later, I find it turning into a wonderful blessing indeed. What seemed to be an adverse condition proves to have been a necessary purification in order to make the blessing possible. I am filled with gratitude and wonder why I was concerned, even temporarily.

By placing my trust in God, my life has been richly blessed with miracles. This is what I mean by the glory of faith.

Common Sense in Religion

*W*e must be careful not to deviate from common sense in religion if we would have true faith. Fanaticism or abnormality results in eccentric behavior. There are people who are inclined to be much impressed by unnatural religious fervor. This is due to ignorance of the spiritual aspects of the universe.

A dogma which causes the followers of one faith to be unfriendly to those of another does not impart the right religious concepts. A true teaching instills the belief that its mission is to serve all people.

The ultimate objective of religion is to assist people to become as nearly as possible the perfect images and likeness of God. While perfection on earth is perhaps beyond the reach of the human self, the sincere effort to attain it is the right attitude and expresses true religious aspiration.

The deeper the faith, the more natural and unaffected a person is. One with true spiritual understanding speaks and acts sensibly, modestly, sincerely. One leaves an uplifting, warm impression upon those with whom one comes in contact. He or she is concerned about the individual happiness of others and the welfare of society. One's true happiness is found in making others happy. This and this alone unlocks the door to God's blessings.

Trust in God Versus Bondage

*T*he importance of placing our faith in divine providence, trusting God implicitly and refraining from worry cannot be over emphasized. This may sound simple and practical, but in application it is not as easy as it appears.

I, too, used to be concerned when I found myself in a dilemma, in spite of my efforts to place my trust in God. It is exceedingly difficult to be completely without anxiety in our materialistic world. However, once I learned implicit faith in divine providence, I was soon able to free myself from all fears.

From a spiritual point of view, worry may be termed a special form of bondage, although few realize it when they are chained to the "worry habit." When we speak of bondage we may also think of covetousness, the inordinate desire for possessions, for luxury, for fame, and so forth. Other types of inordinate attachments are grudges, hatred, vindictiveness, and similar destructive attitudes. In addition, there are worries about and attachments to the past, the present and the future.

Worry is the opposite of trust. It exerts an unfavorable influence upon the outcome of things, for it hinders God's helping, protective hand. The more unrestrained the worry, the more it obstructs divine guidance.

We often prevent our own success. Nearly everyone has experienced an intense desire at one time or other for something which seemed unattainable. After despairing of it and releasing it, it unexpectedly came to pass.

The same sometimes applies to the use of Johrei. When there is an attempt made to help someone, anxiety, in place of trust, can retard progress. But when Johrei is channeled in a true spirit of prayer, without excessive concern, unexpected results are often obtained, even when Johrei is merely being given a trial. When their families or other relatives let anxiety overtake them, the recovery of the critically ill may be impeded; whereas, when Johrei is received with trust, not worry, and with the outcome left in God's hands, the recovery is surprisingly smooth.

Sometimes people who have an intense attachment to physical life feel they can heal themselves when ill, through a strong mental effort;

they often succumb, nevertheless. Their inordinate attachment has been a contributing factor to their transition and indicates the injurious influence of wrong attitudes.

It is best to advise a hopelessly ill person, as well as the family, if possible, that if the physical body does not respond to Johrei, the spiritual body will be purified nevertheless, and this will aid in future spiritual development. Upon surrendering to the will of God, the person frequently improves and ultimately recovers.

In a love relationship, an excessive attachment on the part of either person often produces a reverse effect and causes the other to respond unfavorably. Here, too, the overattachment is responsible for the trouble.

In many cases, the greatest hindrance to progress is an immoderate attachment or concern for the person or thing involved, ironic as this may seem. The world is full of contradictions which complicate our lives but make them interesting as well. It is only through a God-centered way of living that we achieve a balanced outlook and serenity of mind.

Fragments From the Teachings of Meishu-sama

5

Service

Fragments From the Teachings of Meishu-sama

Our Mission

*W*e are born into the earth dimension with the mission of helping to manifest ideal conditions on the planet in accordance with the cosmic plan. When we live and function in harmony with this plan, health, happiness and peace will be intrinsic attributes of daily life. They are our inalienable right.

Unfortunately, because of deviation from the intended pattern, no individual is free of the spiritual clouds passed on from generation to generation, as well as those formed by our own wrong thoughts and actions. In addition, there are the artificial substances harmful to health, wittingly or un-wittingly introduced into the body and increasing the clouds, therefore the suffering. Until we reach the degree of purification that will free us through understanding and wisdom, we will continue to suffer.

However, generally speaking, those whose thoughts and deeds are reflected in service need have no undue anxiety during the transitional period, because they are necessary to the cosmic evolutionary plan.

Purpose of the Divine Light Program

*T*he true mission of Johrei and the work of this organization is to bring about ideal conditions on earth, replacing illness, poverty and strife now prevailing.

Humanity cannot be saved through the restoration of physical health alone. This, therefore, is not the sole purpose of Johrei and of the Divine Light Program.

The ultimate objective is to bring about, by means of the purifying process of Johrei and through service, the necessary spiritual elevation and understanding which make possible the individual's constructive participation in God's plan.

God's Laws and Service

God's immutable laws govern all processes, including the thoughts and actions of people. When our thoughts and actions are creative, beneficial, in harmony with the laws of our being and of the cosmos, they further the evolutionary plan; then we are happy and we prosper. But when we act counter to the laws, we become of little value to ourselves and to God, since God's laws are absolute. When our mental attitude is not in accord with them, we suffer and little can be done for us.

Before I had much spiritual understanding, when I was very ill I used to think, "It would be unfortunate if I were to die. I would not be able to serve in God's cause. I believe God will save me!" God is pleased with self-esteem that is not self-conceit, when it is motivated by the desire to serve God and to fulfill one's destiny in life.

I believe we please God most by serving the lifestream of humanity. We must help as many people as possible to become aware of the divine plan and the Light of God being released for the Age of Light. We must pray for the good of all. To pray only for our own welfare indicates self-centeredness.

When we become effective instruments in the advancement of the cosmic plan, we need not be concerned about our own salvation.

Cosmic Credits

S ometimes people neglect big issues because they are too involved in small ones. This impedes their progress.

Narrow-minded individuals do not expand their thinking very readily. They are often contentious, creating an atmosphere of constraint about them rather than one of freedom and ease. Mental freedom and emotional ease are essential to spiritual well-being and progress, and are in accord with God's law.

People's small faults are not of great significance. More important are their meritorious deeds. A person whose cosmic credits exceed cosmic debits is still ahead, and the divine blessings will be in accordance.

Small individual problems disappear in the big issue of helping to lift humanity at this crucial point in time.

Spiritual Atmosphere

*E*very home, every individual has a spiritual atmosphere.

There are homes which are warm and friendly. Others impart a sense of discomfort, loneliness, even coldness. The atmosphere of each home reflects the attitude of the people who live within it. In one place love and understanding prevail, but in the other home, self-centeredness and lack of consideration prevail.

There are individuals in whose presence we feel a warmth, while others make us feel uncomfortable and ill at ease. It is their mental and spiritual qualities which produce this effect upon us.

Johrei centers are governed by the same principle. Some expand rapidly, others do not. The depth of understanding and the love radiated by the leaders and workers greatly influence the growth of each center. Where there is much love, the Light is intense. People are attracted to it, and the center grows naturally. Location and size have a certain influence, it is true, but its effectiveness is through spiritual communication rather than by the method of presentation. The all-important factor is the genuine love radiating from the persons in charge.

Membership Governed by Spiritual Law

I believe that a person who comes to Johrei is divinely guided and inwardly prompted to do so. It is not necessary for us to advertise our work. Those who are meant to come will come. To rely on advertising would be wrong. If such a method were used in spiritual work, it would become similar to a business venture.

Long ago, there was a dedicated woman who opened a small religious center in Japan. She made no effort to advertise or to do any promotional work. Her friends would urge her to announce the center publicly so people would know about it. But she answered, "God will bring the right ones when the time comes." For two years no one came to hear her. Finally, one person came, then another and another, until eventually the center grew into a large church. This is an example of extraordinary faith, and a significant one. She trusted God implicitly.

A person helped through Johrei will tell friends about it. Gradually, more and more people will come, and they will bring still more people. It is the Light which attracts, a form of divine contagion, so to speak. This is the proper way of expanding our work.

Though we may not comprehend it, God is omniscient. The law of order in the spiritual realm determines who is to come to us and when. However earnestly we might hope for it, an individual will not join us if it is not the proper time to do so. Some people do not become members even though they have observed or experienced beneficial results from Johrei. They may have been dissuaded by relatives or friends who exert an undue influence on them, or they may be prevented by some other adverse condition or circumstance.

Sometimes, people may be thought to be obstacles rather than assets because they appear insincere and even wicked in some cases. If, in truth, they are insincere or wicked, in the plan of God there must be some purpose for their joining, and God will use them nevertheless. There is a law of spiritual relationship which governs those who enter or join the Johrei path of Light.

The question has been asked as to whether there is an effective way to convert an atheist. There is no special method. A person can be led to Johrei through hearing about it or through reading its literature, whether or not the person is an atheist. Our part is to pray with sincerity and devotion for the furthering of God's plan and leave the results to God.

Beyond telling those who are in need of help and Johrei about our work, we need not be unduly concerned. There is always a proper time for each individual to come. When that time arrives, the person will appear on his or her own initiative. The time factor is a mysterious thing, difficult for us to determine.

Be Guided in Expanding the Work

Sometimes Johrei members become concerned when, contrary to their expectations, expansion is slow. Instead of waiting patiently, they try to promote the work by coercive methods. Often those who rely upon human judgment alone are unsuccessful in their effort to make others understand the basic aims of the Johrei movement. They forget that their own spiritual development is of primary importance and that the work is to be left to God's guidance. When God-directed, there is no distress connected with the activity.

Since ancient times missionary work has been replete with suffering. Especially in Christianity, we find many cases of actual martyrdom. Its missionaries made great effort to propagate the teachings of Jesus, some risking their lives in uncivilized areas such as are found in certain parts of Africa. This indeed showed a valiant spirit, but many suffered and sacrificed themselves needlessly.

Religious history, so filled with tales of hardship, established the idea that suffering is inevitable. There may be people who strain unduly in attempting to do their part. The more they strain, the more they subject themselves to disappointing experiences.

Coercion and overzealous methods were used during the Age of Darkness. Johrei belongs to the Age of Light. Seers of old prophesied the advent of heaven on earth, although they did not mention how it was to come about. Johrei is dedicated to this end.

We are now in the dawn of the Age of Light, and the time has come for us to do our part as God's co-workers, to help fulfill the plan for establishing an ideal world in which love, understanding and happiness prevail. This change must first take place within the mind and heart of each person. Each must establish a happy, heavenly state of mind within himself or herself. This state will then be reflected upon the family, the environment and the country. In time it will spread the world over, and heaven on earth will become a reality.

There is nothing heavenly about laboriousness or suffering. In the service of channeling Johrei, for instance, there are homes to which we go with delight, and we are blessed with wonderful results. Then there may be others to which we go with a feeling of reluctance, accomplishing little. As a rule, if we cannot go in a spirit of cheerfulness or joy, it is better not to go at all. Of course, this must not become a matter of self-decision. After we reach a certain degree of spiritual awareness, we will always look to God for guidance.

Impulsive human effort often produces tension in ourselves and in others. It is good to make plans. We cannot accomplish anything worthwhile without them, but often we try to force them into realization, with adverse results. When we are guided by God's laws rather than by human intellect, our progress is rapid beyond any possible expectation.

Aware of this truth, whenever something is not going right I stop and release the entire matter into God's hands. When I come back to the problem, it works out favorably.

We must follow this principle in Johrei work. It then becomes a simple, heaven-directed way of life.

Do Not Be Too Easygoing

*E*mphasis on leaving everything in God's hands is not to be understood as meaning that we may let things go without doing our part, taking for granted that God will do everything for us. Rather, it means not to depend upon our human intellect and conviction only, but to seek to be guided by God's wisdom in all that we do.

It is essential to have an open, flexible mind and to keep a balanced outlook. Whether we employ the *Daijo* or the *Shojo* approach, we must not be dogmatic, but, using both, must always come back to the central point, or *Izunome*.

[Please see the next chapter for a description of the italicized words.]

Rely on God

W hen we pray sincerely with all our hearts and souls, place our lives in God's hands, and do our best to serve God and humanity, we will radiate the qualities that lead others to the pathway of Light.

God's Co-Workers

W hen channeling Johrei, it is important to avoid undue eagerness, impatience, tension and haste. Also, it is not at all right to offer help in illness or misfortune with the thought that it will serve to advertise Johrei. In a business undertaking this might work, but ulterior motives are counter to a God-directed plan.

Our work does not expand in this manner nor generally through people with a large circle of acquaintances. Rather, word of it often spreads unexpectedly through very inconspicuous people. God's ways are very different, and often they are quite contrary to our concepts. The plans of people must be subservient to God's plan.

When a person comes to receive Johrei, even though this person may appear to be insignificant, we must think of him or her as being God-sent. Should a well-known or influential individual come for Johrei, let us not think, "This person must be helped at any cost because he or she can help us." We must serve the Light without bias. Inconspicuous people often prove to be spiritually advanced souls.

If a person receiving Johrei is persuaded to stop, we must not interfere. It may be God's plan for this person for the time being.

Dogmatic opinions and refusal to listen to what others may have to say does not reflect true serenity of mind.

Those with higher understanding can turn to the right as easily as to the left, as the need arises. They are the ones prepared to carry forward this work.

6

Daijo, Shojo, Izunome

Fragments From the Teachings of Meishu-sama

Daijo, Shojo, Izunome

aijo illustrates the horizontal aspects of life, *shojo* the vertical. Daijo is like the activity of water, which endlessly spreads horizontally. Shojo is of the activity of fire. It is narrow, burns deep, and flames high. It unites humanity with God. Daijo unites person with person.

The shojo principle is narrow and uncompromising. The lives of people of a shojo disposition are regulated by standards which are often strict and rigid. Also, shojo people tend to be more critical of others and term things "good" or "bad."

The daijo principle is horizontally inclusive. People of a daijo disposition, in general, are liberal and quite open to change. On the other hand, they may have a tendency to be too liberal and to lack spiritual orientation and depth.

Izunome symbolizes the balanced cross, indicating the perfect blending of the vertical and the horizontal principles.

Until the present day, the East stood for the vertical, the West for the horizontal. During the Age of Night the providence of God established the spiritual realm in this way. This is why some Eastern cultures cherished the idea of ancestor reverence, the virtue of loyalty and filial piety. This is why they maintained a strict class system.

In the West affection between husband and wife formed the keynote, expanding to love for other people, for all of humanity.

Christianity is daijo and so has spread the world over. It stresses love for others, an activity on a horizontal level.

Buddhism is shojo and is mainly contained within specific groups. It stresses meditation for wisdom and self-realization. This activity is vertical—high and deep. This tends to send its disciples into seclusion.

The East adhering to the vertical and the West to the horizontal, there has been little understanding between the two, which has often given rise to conflicts.

However, the time is at hand for the vertical and the horizontal principles to merge and form the balanced cross, Izunome. A happy unification of the Eastern and Western civilizations will be the result. Only then can humanity enter the ideal state of true civilization and experience Paradise on Earth. The Johrei movement makes us aware that it can be accomplished by the Light of God.

We must be flexible and respond to the demands of a given situation, sometimes adhering to the shojo principle, sometimes applying the daijo method, but always coming back to the center point, Izunome. Daijo, in the broader, truer sense, is all inclusive and so includes shojo. Generally speaking, having shojo deep within as the guiding principle, it is good to act in a daijo way.

However, daijo alone can be dangerous. Young people especially may tend to become too self-indulgent. Shojo establishes the vertical spiritual principle, in which all need to be grounded before entering the daijo principle of horizontal expansion. In this way one may reach the perfect balance of the two, or the balanced cross, Izunome.

[Note: *Daijo* 大乗

Shojo 小乗

Izunome 伊都能売

are Japanese words for which there are no exact equivalents in English.]

73

"Good" and "Evil" Are Relative

There are natural laws in the universe which govern all processes and all change. These laws also govern religion, philosophy, science, politics, education, economics, art, peace and war, good and evil, and so forth.

When we conform to these natural, self-regulatory laws our way is smoother. When we go counter to them difficulties arise.

People of daijo thinking speak less of "good" or "evil" or of the mistakes of others than people of shojo thinking. Since "good" and "evil" are relative terms in a given situation, we cannot truly judge the actions of others but need to apply the broad-mindedness of daijo thinking in all our relationships.

When we think and act in accordance with God's immutable laws which govern all creation, all action, the results are beneficial. Regardless of the opinions of people, it is the end result which counts.

Conflict Between "Good" and "Evil"

*T*he domain of God is too profound for ordinary human understanding. Especially bewildering and trying is the continuous conflict between that which humanity terms "good" and that which humanity feels is "evil." Yet, "good" and "evil" are relative, and we cannot draw hasty conclusions as to the good or the bad of things. Often evil forces, distressing as they may be, serve as a means of soul discipline, to develop strength in constructive, creative, capable people. In this sense, they constitute something like a rubstone and serve a beneficial end.

Good is destined to triumph ultimately, otherwise life on earth would be completely dominated by evil, and both humanity and the planet would perish.

During the Nocturnal Age the destructive forces often won over the constructive forces temporarily. This reflected upon the physical world in the form of misfortunes, disasters, and all sorts of miseries, affecting the welfare of seemingly good people. However, now that the Age of Light is dawning, the nature of evil will gradually become evident and lose power. The divine forces will gain the upper hand and will establish new and beneficial social conditions.

One of the characteristics of evil forces is their persistence. Win or lose, they never give up. This continues the refining and strengthening of the constructive. In the Age of Light there will still be negative forces, but they will have little power.

In speaking of our struggle with evil, let me stress two things: one, do not be afraid of dark forces; two, do not criticize others as "instruments" of evil forces. We cannot be certain they are, and in judging them we encroach upon the domain of God. We must use wisdom and proceed according to each individual situation. If necessary, we must withdraw rather than "push" our way. Even if evil seems to win for a while, in the end it will lose.

In the Age of Light, when the constructive forces have completely taken control and have displaced the destructive, Paradise on Earth will be realized.

Judge Not...

"Judge not" is a subject which bears repetition.

There are people who think and speak of others as being "good" or "evil." On occasion they go so far as to say that some are possessed of evil spirits. People cannot know the good or evil, right or wrong in others. This wisdom belongs to the domain of God. God alone is able to judge. It is conceit that causes people to assume the right to pass judgment upon others.

There are persons who condemn other people's faiths. There are members who feel some of our branches need reorganization. We should be very cautious when dealing with situations of this nature. People who labor under misconceptions often become guilty of interfering with the working out of a cosmic pattern. We must keep in mind that the Supreme God presides over all, and God's wisdom is too profound for superficial understanding. It is wise to hold strictly to the injunction, "Judge not that ye be not judged," if we desire to lead God-centered lives.

On Love

Generally speaking, there are two kinds of love: the universal, all-inclusive love of God, and the individualized love of people, which is limited.

Shojo love, as a rule, is more personalized and, when extreme, may limit itself to love of self, family, friends, one's own group or class and one's country. While good in itself, it is somewhat limited and so may assume selfish ends and turn into a self-centered love. The more intense it is, the more it can become a source of injustice and conflict, and, in its worst political aspects, lead to war.

Daijo love is broader and more encompassing, and in this respect more nearly resembles universal love, which includes all humanity. In its highest and finest sense, it may be trusted more fully than a circumscribed shojo love. The perfect balance of universal love should prevail and become the common ideal of people everywhere.

We hear of strife between religious sects and of wars in the name of religion. Our ideal is a religion that works hand in hand with other religions to create a world of love and peace, not only advocating but exemplifying universal love.

Broadmindedness

*T*he statement that what is good from the shojo standpoint is bad from that of daijo, and vice versa, requires reflection. Objectively speaking, a shojo-type person may go to extremes which limit reflection and common sense. This type of person is often eccentric and dogmatic. This person will criticize others more quickly and term things either "good" or "evil," whereas daijo implies that a person looks at things from a broad viewpoint.

Without the horizontally balancing principle of daijo, shojo people may place too much confidence in their own ability and judgment, and apply themselves too earnestly and onesidedly to their undertakings. They may even forget to depend on divine power and assistance. This prevents their becoming really successful.

Japan was an example of shojo thinking at the time of World War II. The whole nation fought madly, risking everything. The good those in command sought for their country was based on ambition and self-love. They were interested only in their own prosperity, regardless of other countries. Had Japan acted from a balanced daijo point of view, it would not have entered into an aggressive war, and it would have won the love and respect of the rest of the world. It would then have enjoyed peace and prosperity instead of ignominious defeat. Worldwide good alone is enduring.

In contrast to God's universal love, humanity's love is limited and often harmful in its ultimate conclusion.

Because daijo people are more outgoing in their relationships with others, they are often more successful without having to expend any great effort.

Understanding the difference between the horizontal daijo and the vertical shojo viewpoints, we must try to bring the two into balance at their central point, or Izunome. People will naturally be attracted to us and will desire to cooperate with us when we are free of criticism and show encompassing good will.

Love of Humanity
Is Love of Life

Often the difference in religious attitude between shojo and daijo people is that shojo people are inclined to think in terms of their individual salvation, while daijo people are more given to think of the deliverance of others also.

People frequently seek only their own happiness, their own advancement. However high their aspirations may be, this attitude indicates undue self-love, and cannot be greatly blessed by God. True religious concern includes all others. When we forget ourselves in responding to the needs of others, we truly live our faith. This is our greater salvation, for we cannot be truly happy while others suffer.

Those with shojo religious tendencies sometimes resent the slightest remark or criticism directed against them. Their resentment results in unhappiness to themselves, and it is not pleasing to God. They must pray to be shown the way. To love and help others is true religion and true love of life.

Freedom in Religion

The general concept among nonreligious people appears to be that religion restricts freedom. Many individuals fear that they might have to observe rigid rules and regulations, which causes them to avoid religious affiliation. This mistaken idea springs from shojo attitudes in some of the existing religions. Religions of shojo tendency are usually based on the belief that only asceticism will bring spiritual awakening. This may lead their devotees to live lives of suffering, which, from our point of view, is a misleading idea. We believe that we can achieve an awakened spiritual state through the Light of God without unnecessary suffering.

Shojo concepts, stemming from Brahmanism in India, attribute redemption to self-discipline, while daijo concepts consider that inner emancipation can be attained by relying on the "Power from on High," making possible joy and serenity of mind.

There is little freedom in shojo. There is freedom in daijo, but it needs to be restrained. Unless wisdom is used, too much self-indulgence results. Freedom at the expense of others is license, which produces a guilt complex and robs us of serenity of mind. Respect for the equal rights of others leads to true freedom and true happiness.

Be a Good Listener

*A*n ancient Chinese philosopher once said, "Don't underestimate people when they talk to you." What he meant was that we should listen with open minds and not discount a person's ideas before we know what the person has to say; that we must not judge by appearances. We can often learn something valuable from an illiterate laborer or a simple farmer.

Many times we hear a small child voice a wonderful truth or express an original idea. Bergson, in his book *Intuition*, states that children are keenly intuitive and often speak right to the point. In arguments between mother and child, we frequently find the truth to be on the child's side.

I make it a point to listen to the people who work under my direction, and to let them have their way as much as possible. Even when they insist on some silly idea, I try to give in whenever I can. Only when I feel that wrong attitudes are influencing the situation am I adamant. Some fear a loss of dignity or prestige if they listen to their subordinates. This is absurd.

Even when a person is saying something you believe untrue, it is not wise to reject it immediately and insist on your point or to censure the person. Although you know the person is telling a lie, appear undisturbed by it. This is permissible if you are sincere and true within your own heart.

Sometimes an art dealer has come to me with an imitation, hoping to deceive me into buying it. As I listen, once in a while I find something uplifting and useful mixed in with the garrulous fabrication.

Yield That
You May Conquer

"Be flexible to conquer" is a golden rule. It may be difficult to practice but we need to try to train our tempers and school our minds in this way. In some cases it may be better to be misunderstood or to lose an argument. It is good character training, and any possible humiliation is only in the mind and is temporary.

As time goes on, the other person concerned may begin to understand the true situation with a change of attitude being the result. The other person may think, "That is a real person," and begin to trust and admire you. Or, your opponent seemingly having won the argument, becomes uncertain, realizing he or she has no idea what you have in mind. Thus the loser becomes the winner, and that is why it is sometimes better to let the other person have his or her way.

To adhere only to our own opinions is an unwise policy. Even though we may be right we need not necessarily persist in having our own way. If we learn to yield in a given situation we will win in the end, provided we stand for what is right and true.

Often when people engage in something important they think it will require effort, strain and concentration. When under strain our inner power becomes limited, whereas when we are relaxed it can flow unrestricted. The same principle holds true in Johrei. The more relaxed in mind and hand, the more attuned we are, and the more effective the Johrei.

General McArthur knew when and how to retreat in a battle. As a rule, a soldier who knows how to retreat is a great leader. To keep on at undue risk is poor policy. It is not true courage. What counts is the end result.

Many persons experience results contrary to their expectations, because the way of the world in general is quite foreign to the way of truth.

When I started the Johrei movement, it was my policy to tell people to work in as quiet and unobtrusive a manner as possible. Some advised me to advertise, but I did not do so. Many people are inclined to pursue worldly, temporary things, the same as they seek temporary relief in illness. In a truly spiritual work, we must aim at the true and the eternal so we may be prepared for the future.